The School Psychology Licensure Exam Guide

The School Psychology Licensure Exam Guide

The Most Effective Guide to Prepare for the National Association of School Psychologists (NASP) Exam

Peter Thompson, M.Ed., Ed.S.

iUniverse, Inc.
New York Lincoln Shanghai

The School Psychology Licensure Exam Guide
The Most Effective Guide to Prepare for the National Association of School Psychologists (NASP) Exam

iUniverse books may be ordered through booksellers or by contacting:

iUniverse
2021 Pine Lake Road, Suite 100
Lincoln, NE 68512
www.iuniverse.com
1-800-Authors (1-800-288-4677)

ISBN: 0-595-33527-6

Printed in the United States of America

ACKNOWLEDGMENTS

I would like to express my sincerest gratitude to two people who directly helped me with this guide. Dr. Colette Hohnbaum is not only a practicing school psychologist, but also an outstanding professor. Colette is one of the most skilled and personable psychologists in the state of Colorado. Her insight and advice continue to be invaluable to me.

Beth Henson is an attorney of extraordinary acumen. I am indebted to her for the time she spent helping me. I wish her and her new family a lifetime of joy.

Finally, I thank my wife and daughter for their love and support. I can never say enough times how much they mean to me.

CONTENTS

INTRODUCTION

*What lies behind us and what lies before us are tiny matters
compared to what lies within us.*
—*Ralph W. Emerson*

When preparing to tackle the licensure exam for school psychology (*the exam*), I diligently gathered as many resources as I could find. I queried several professors, investigated the Internet and pooled information from various study groups. During this time, I was absolutely flabbergasted and dismayed at the paucity of information available to help me study.

Soon, my anxiety surrounding this vital test evolved into dread. After all, you could have stellar grades in graduate school, but if you fail this one crucial exam there would be no license to practice. In other words, I believed this one test held the key to my occupational future. As it turned out, the exam's tough reputation and my thinking were faulty. The hype surrounding the test was just that—-hype.

If you are a few months away from taking the licensure exam, your primary enemy is probably anxiety. As future psychologists, we know that fear is born out of a lack of control or understanding of unknown events. Therefore, instead of letting your emotions detract from your abilities, harness the energy provided by this emotion to direct your actions to overcome the unknown (re-read the above quote). Additionally, you must moderate your worries by keeping in mind that the majority of people will pass the licensure exam and you *can* always retake the test.

School psychology is built upon the simple tenet of helping others in need. Consequently, this guide endeavors to help future psychologists enter this worthy field. While this guide is not all encompassing, I firmly believe that its information will assist aspiring school psychologists prepare for the exam. However, it is critical to understand that no single book or source holds all of the answers. The reader must utilize every resource possible and this book is just one piece of the preparation pie.

Finally, there is a valuable concept I would like you to remember. The majority of test takers will soon be practitioners employed by large public school districts. Every year, millions of young students will also take important standardized tests that are just as stressful to them. If empathy is the hallmark trait of our profession, then let your test experience stew just a bit so you can truly understand how your future clients feel when you administer a formal assessment.

I wish the reader good luck not only taking the exam but also in making a positive change in the lives of children.

CHAPTER ONE

The Exam and General Advice

The chief benefit of this book is that it provides a general idea of what to expect on the National Association of School Psychologists (NASP) licensure exam. When people understand what to expect and have a strategy on how to approach a task, their anxiety will decrease. Additionally, when emotions are tamed, clarity of thought emerges and more cognitive energy can be devoted to higher order reasoning.

I have found the primary source of stress surrounding this test is the mystery of the content and how to study for it. Trying to study for a comprehensive standardized psychology test is like studying for a history test——it is incalculably broad. The range of topics is so vast it seems overwhelming to start studying. However, the following chapter contains suggestions and information that can help you organize an effective approach to the exam.

The following suggestions are based on remarks and observations from people who have taken the exam. Also, some ideas and advice are from practicing school psychologists. The example items are not identical to the actual test questions, but are highly similar in content and format. Some suggestions might be more useful than others. However, all advice and examples (even obvious ones) have been provided due to the various needs of different test takers. Also, it is extremely important to bear in mind that any statements made in this book are founded upon educated opinion. Even though the advice is given out of sincerity, the veracity of any comment needs to be checked by the reader if questioned. Remember, psychology is a dynamic and evolving field of study. Therefore, theories, best practices and professional positions can change with time.

The Test Format

The NASP exam is administered through the Praxis series of tests (a well-known testing business). The school psychology exam consists of 120 multiple choice questions and lasts roughly two hours within a tightly controlled setting. Typically, each question has four response choices. A few questions might have five choices.

While specific details about test construction and scoring are difficult to ascertain, it appears there are multiple versions of this exam. Most likely, a large pool of questions are used to construct different tests. In other words, the test changes with every group administration. While you might have a few identical items on your test as a person from a previous group, it is unlikely you will get the same overall test from a prior administration.

The content areas of the test are *generally* broken down into five domains. As the actual NASP test varies from each administration, so do the number of questions asked that are associated with each domain area. On your exam, you might have more or fewer questions asked regarding each category. Also, keep in mind that all domains may share similar content and therefore specific test items could be placed in more than one domain. For example, a test question could ask about an intervention strategy that relies on general psychological principles; thus, that particular question has its roots in two domains (intervention and general psychological principles).

General Domains of the NASP Exam Format

1. Assessments, Diagnosis and Identification-------------25% (25–30 items)

2. Intervention and Prevention---------------------------25% (25–30 items)

3. General Psychological Principles----------------------20% (20–25 items)

4. Education Principles/Methods--------------------10–15% (10–15 items)

5. Legal and Ethics----------------------------------15–18% (20–25 items)

> **Assessment/Identification** questions regard behavioral and cognitive assessment. These questions are typically straightforward and factual. For example, you might be asked which subtest on the WISC-IV is not appropriate for visually impaired students.

> **Prevention and Intervention** questions center on counseling techniques, theories and crisis intervention. Some questions are geared toward special education population or specific strategies regarding individual intervention. Example—Which strategies are used to help

a student with assertiveness issues? (Answer—modeling and rehearsal).

➤ **General Psychological Principles** questions regard general principles related to psychometric testing and the field of psychology. A question within this domain might ask, "Which stage of Erik Erikson's psycho-social developmental theory addresses the middle childhood years (6–12 years old)?" The answer is Stage Four—Industry v. Inferiority.

➤ **Educational psychology** questions tend to focus on teaching practices and classroom management techniques. This domain might also cover consultation models. People who have little teaching experience might find this area challenging. An example question might be, "What is an effective method to teach and build comprehension skills?" Answer—Have students ask themselves questions (self-talk) while reading a passage and to predict the outcome. It is important to remember that this particular domain may have similar questions as the general psychology or intervention domains.

➤ **Legal and Ethical** questions are sometimes given within a brief case study or vignette format. Be familiar not only with specific case law (landmark rulings), but also the ramifications of the outcomes of such rulings. Many questions are also based on the Individual Disability Education Act (IDEA).

General Suggestions for Studying and Preparing

1. Start studying early for the test. Some people study a week before the test and soon realize that this was not enough time due to the vastness of the subject area. In my opinion, it is best to study *at least* a month prior to the test. Your first few days will entail collecting and organizing information and notes. If you study one or two hours a day for a month, this will provide you with an adequate foundation. Also, there is some research that suggests studying before going to sleep is more effective than studying during the stress of the daytime.

2. Organize your notes and information according to the five broad categories listed previously.

3. Develop keyword and general concept lists. I found this tip to be extremely helpful. Such lists make reviewing very time efficient and effective.

4.   Study general concepts and keywords more than specific facts. "Familiarize" more than "memorize." Although you certainly have to memorize some facts (case law, certain psychometric properties, psychological theories), understanding broad concepts provides a foundation to answer the most questions. For example, NASP's position on grade retention is that the practice is not a good idea in most cases. Your question on the test will usually be in the form of an example, "A parent comes to you and tells you her son has failed three classes in seventh grade and wants to retain him; what is your response?" In such a case, your response should be to determine if something is interfering with the child's learning (social, emotional problems, learning difficulties) and suggest various options for the child to make up the subjects (summer school). Notice how the previous question does not explicitly ask about NASP's position on grade retention.

5.   Create or join a study group. Study groups are effective if they are <u>kept small</u> (3–4 people). With too many people, focusing the group and socializing become issues. Do not overemphasize study groups. Meet just a few times with the group to exchange information and quiz each other. Everyone within the small group should bring completed outlines and notes to the first meeting. Group members should have copies of their outlines to share. Although this is more work than dividing tasks up between individual members, information gathered this way is more comprehensive and usually stimulates meaningful conversations about relevant test items.

6.   Secure an undergraduate "Introduction to Psychology" textbook and read the summaries for each chapter. The textbook should be no more than five years old. Such textbooks are excellent for reviewing the newest general psychological theories and research. Additionally, these books are easy to digest and key concepts are presented in a thorough manner.

7.   Study your weak content areas, but be careful how you emphasize any one area. I spent most of my time studying specific case laws. I did this at the expense of other information that I thought I knew. On my specific exam, I did not have one single direct case law question, but I had several psychometric questions instead. If you feel you are weak in one of the five domain areas, by all means spend a little more time to bolster your weakness. However, do not skimp on studying an area because you think it is your strength.

8. Read chapter summaries from major textbooks you purchased during your program of study. Again, be very familiar with broad concepts and memorize only "key" facts. Be very judicious in what you decide to memorize. Do not spend too much time reading entire chapters unless you are very weak in that area. Recommended authors of well-known textbooks include Jerome Sattler—his books on cognitive and behavioral assessments and Randy Kamphaus for similar information.

9. Read chapter summaries and abstracts from NASP's *Best Practices in School Psychology*. Many graduate students attempt to read the entire best practices book. While this is useful, it is highly time-consuming and large sections will not be on the test. After speaking with colleagues who took the exam, they told me that reading the summaries and a few specific chapters was most effective. I found reading chapters that dealt with multi-cultural issues, testing, interventions (counseling) and consultation to be helpful.

10. Be familiar with key acronyms. You do not necessarily have to memorize them, but be able to recognize an acronym and be familiar with its importance.

11. Take as many practice tests as possible and discuss missed items with your study group. If you have an effective study group, have each member create a mini-test. Swap tests and discuss them at your next session. Taking practice tests is the best way to initially reduce test anxiety. It will also prepare your mind for taking timed tests.

12. When taking the exam, practice effective time management. To my knowledge, all questions are scored equally. Therefore, do not spend too much time on any one particular item. There are 120 questions to answer in two hours. I am a slow test taker and had 15 minutes to spare.

13. Bring several extra pencils with high quality erasers to the test.

14. Never leave any question unanswered. Usually, you will be able to quickly narrow down your test answer to two choices. If you have difficulty with choosing an answer, put a small mark by the question and give it a good guess. If time permits at the end, go back and examine the marked question again (there is some debate about whether a person's first guess is the most accurate).

15. Allow yourself time at the end of the test to check your answers. If you have been taking practice tests, you should have honed your time management skills. If you have extra time when you complete your test, you

should do two things. First, review the entire test and make sure each oval within the multiple-choice format is cleanly filled. Stray marks or messy corrections might interfere with scoring—this is very important. Second, reread the questions you had difficulty answering and see if other test items might provide help. During my test, I noticed that one test item contained information that helped answer another item that I had trouble answering.

16. Go to the NASP Internet site and read about NASP's position papers and best practices.

17. If you are going to take a blind guess answering a question, some of my colleagues suggest that it is best to guess "C" or "D." However, if I can match a keyword in the choice section to anything in the question, I usually answer accordingly.

18. Register to take the test as early as possible. The test is sponsored by Praxis and you will be able to register through the Internet. If you do not register early, you run the risk of not being able to take the test in a convenient location. Some people might have to drive a very long distance to take the test. Remember to double-check your University's code that you will have to enter. If you put the wrong code, your school will not receive your scores. A few weeks after the test, a copy of your scores are sent to your home and a breakdown of how you performed on each section of the test will be detailed.

19. Allow yourself to miss a few questions without stressing about it. Remember, you can miss several items and still pass the test. Do not be a perfectionist or think you have to know it all. For practical purposes, there is no difference between getting 70% correct and 100% correct— both scores pass and nobody asks you your scores after you graduate.

20. When studying general psychological theories and concepts, focus on those parts that are relevant only to the 5–18 years-old age group. For example, be more familiar with Erikson's psychosocial stages for children than for the adults.

21. On the test day, relax, relax and relax. Your emotions and anxiety will be elevated on the day you take the test. Some anxiety is helpful, but not too much. If you have sincerely prepared for the test, then do not second guess your efforts—you ARE prepared. Follow your normal routine the day of the test. Always remember that you can re-take the test if you do not perform as well as you expect. In fact, some people study for the

NASP test by taking it twice. When I took the test, I told myself beforehand that I would show up about a half-hour early and only review keywords and concepts. After reviewing once, that was it. I simply enjoyed my coffee and waited for the test to begin.

22. Finally, eat a decent dinner and get a "full" night's sleep before the test. The day before the exam, review your notes, but do not stress or try to learn new material. It is important to hydrate yourself by drinking an extra glass of water. The brain needs water to think effectively.

Observations from *my* NASP exam

➤ My test had 15 large scenario-type questions. Scenario questions are an 8–12 sentence paragraph. After reading this small paragraph, you have to choose the best answer from 4–5 choices.

➤ Of the 15 scenario questions, 3 or 4 of these scenarios had multiple questions attached to it. For example, one vignette accounted for questions numbered 65–68.

➤ Several questions on the exam were about 1 to 3 short sentences in length. These questions asked for straightforward information. For example, Carl Rogers is best known for what?

➤ Approximately 75% of the questions, I was able to very quickly narrow the choices down to 2 responses. The two narrowed-down responses seemed to have kernels of truth in both of them. Take the best educated guess and look for keywords that match your answer to the question.

➤ Roughly 65% of the questions were short example type that asks you to apply your knowledge. For example, "You have a new student that was referred for anxiety problems around test taking. What should you do first?" Answer—secure signed permission from the parents to counsel the student.

➤ I completed the test with about 15 minutes to spare. I consider myself a moderately fast test taker. I estimated about 66% of my colleagues were finished before me.

➤ It seemed 2 or 3 questions on the exam helped to answer a few other items because of the information they contained. Sometimes keywords in the choices will remind you of concepts and other important ideas.

➤ Very few, if any, items had tricky or multiple answers. For example, I did not have answer choices that read "A and C are true."

CHAPTER TWO

Psycho-educational Concepts and Ideas to Help with Studying

By no means does this chapter contain everything you need to know. The field of psychology is far too broad to cover with just one book. As school psychologists, we are busy practitioners who must keep abreast of several new developments within the various subfields of psychology. We must know concepts in neuropsychology, counseling psychology, social psychology, educational psychology and other branches of our discipline.

Despite the vastness of the psychological arena, this chapter provides some of the principles and specific facts the reader needs for a starting point and foundation to prepare for the NASP exam. Again, I must emphasize that multiple streams of information is the best approach in your studies.

The following items were taken from a wide range of resources. Each concept and theory has several other ideas attached to it. Therefore, any one concept can spawn numerous questions from it. For example, the single theory of Behaviorism has B.F. Skinner associated with it as well as dozens of other crucial concepts. Behaviorism includes concepts such as schedules of reinforcement, extinction, Premack principle and punishment. When reviewing any mainstream psychological theory, let it stimulate your thinking about associated ideas and possible test questions. In other words, the reader is strongly encouraged to expand and acquire supplemental information on several of the concepts presented in this chapter.

My last piece of advice involves the efficient use of time and the allocation of cognitive energy. Undoubtedly, if you earnestly study for a month prior to your NASP exam, you will inadvertently memorize specific concepts. Indeed, some key ideas need to be memorized such as major "stage" theories and landmark educational laws. However, as stated previously, it is beneficial to be "highly familiar" with many concepts rather than expending energy memorizing a mountain of specific facts. The majority of the exam asks you to *apply* your knowledge, rather than spit back psychological trivia.

The following section delineates some key ideas and important points to study from the five major domains the NASP exam purportedly has for its structure. Again, the five areas are:

I.   Assessments, Diagnostic and Identification

II.   Intervention and Prevention

III. General Psychological Principles

IV.   Education Principles/Methods

V.   Legal and Ethics

I. Assessments and Identification

1.   Many concepts nested under this domain may include questions regarding identifying students with particular disabilities, or specific questions regarding psychological tests and their administration. Although psychometric and statistical information is typically found within "General Psychological Principles," be prepared to *apply* such information regarding student assessments.

2.   "Best practice" suggests that school psychologists use multiple sources of information to identify children with disabilities or problems. Although standardized cognitive assessments are central in the assessment process, such IQ tests cannot be used in isolation. Both *formal* and *informal* measures should be utilized to support or supplement decisions.

3.   Be familiar with the major types of behavioral observational methods used in an emotional or behavioral assessment. Some common observational methods include narrative, interval, event and ratings recording. The narrative method provides broad and narrow information from running records. Interval recording uses time sampling techniques. Event recording documents the target behavior as it occurs. Last, the ratings method uses rankings (such as 1–5) to evaluate global characteristics of a person.

4. Be familiar with the sources of error typically associated with behavioral assessments. For example, many behavioral surveys may have observer or rater bias. When evaluating behavior assessments, one must study the percentage of agreement between raters. Also, observers should sample behavior more than once to increase reliability.

5. Observers during an assessment can be influenced by the "halo effect," fatigue and personal biases.

6. Know the particular characteristics of several common behavioral/emotional assessments. Some common social/emotional assessments include the BASC, MMPI, APS, Conners (for ADHD), and the Beck Depression Scales. A question on the NASP test might ask, "Which test is used to evaluate inattention in children?" The answer in this case is the Conners ADHD Scales.

7. Know how projective measures, such as the Rorsharch, are used. Typically, such measures are used as a supplemental part of a battery of psychological tests. Also, understand the benefits and limitations of projective assessments (such as low psychometric reliability).

8. Be familiar with common adaptive/functional assessments such as the Vineland and the Adaptive Behavior Assessment System (ABAS). Most school districts suggest that Standard Scores on adaptive assessments and intelligence tests should be two (2) Standard Deviations below the mean to identify children with mental retardation. (SS< 70)

9. Know the steps in conducting a Functional Behavioral Assessment (Analyis), or FBA. The primary steps in a FBA include determining the **antecedents** of the behavior, the target **behavior** itself and the **consequence** for the behavior. To help remember this general outline, think of A-B-C.

10. When analyzing a behavior, a psychologist should pay particular attention to the **intensity, frequency** and **duration** of the behavior. The three previous characteristics of the behavioral analysis must show a significant negative impact on the student's classroom performance and/or social development in order to qualify for special education.

11. Two main functions of a behavior are either to gain something positive or escape something negative. In addition, cognitive-behaviorists believe that attention, power/control, affiliation and revenge are key reasons for behavior.

12. Although usually found within the "Interventions" domain, be familiar with how to use your assessment data to write an intervention plan. Remember to include positive strategies and a replacement behavior for the negative behavior in your plan.

13. Bell Curve/Normal Curve—represents normative information about typical human traits. The Normal Curve is based on a large population of people and reflects typical human conditions. 68% of people comprise the bulk (center) of the Bell Curve. Most standardized cognitive assessments are predicated on the Normal Curve theory.

14. Fluid Intelligence—the ability to solve problems through reasoning. Fluid problem solving is not primarily based on previously learned facts, techniques or language. Fluid reasoning is sometimes referred to as nonverbal reasoning, immediate problem solving or simultaneous processing. Fluid thinking involves the ability to summarize and comprehend information to solve a task.

15. Crystallized Intelligence is the ability to solve problems by applying learned facts and language. The verbal sections of IQ tests illustrate this type of intelligence. Catell and Horn are the chief theorists behind the fluid and crystallized intelligence model.

16. Emotional intelligence is the ability to be aware of one's emotions, regulate one's emotions and accurately read the emotions of others. Current research in this area shows that students with low emotional and social intelligence have undesirable life outcomes.

17. Be familiar with the different types of disorders, their causes and prevalence rates. It is imperative to study broad identification characteristics of disorders as well as their "best practice" for intervention. Major disorders to study are Learning Disorders (10–15% of a population), Autism (Pervasive Developmental Disorder—5 per 10,000 people with male to female ratio about 4:1), Asperger's Syndrome, Language Disorders, Attention Deficit Hyperactivity Disorder (ADHD-both inattentive and hyperactivity types; 3–7% of the population), Down Syndrome, Fragile X, Mental Retardation and tic disorders.

18. Authentic assessments are becoming popular. These types of dynamic assessments usually have the student perform a typical classroom task (such as reading). Sometimes, these tasks take place in the actual environment in which the behavior is normally seen.

19. When interpreting the results of major cognitive tests, it is best practice to start at the broadest level, then narrow your interpretation to the subtest level. The most valid score is usually the full scale score, followed by the major domain or cluster scores. Item analysis is least reliable, but may reveal important information.

20. Know factors that can interfere with obtaining accurate test results. Some major factors include motivation, fatigue, undisclosed vision or hearing difficulties and stress.

21. Know the uses and key characteristics for major cognitive assessments.

    Wechsler Intellegence Scale for Children (WISC-III): This test is being replaced by the WISC-IV. The WISC-III is largely supported by the Catell-Horn model of Crystallized and Fluid intelligence. It has a broad Verbal and Performance domain. The Performance domain assess abstract reasoning and motor skills.

    WISC-IV: The WISCl-IV assesses five broad domains—Verbal, Perceptual, Memory, Processing Speed and Executive Function. Age range is 6 years old to 16:11.

    Weschsler Preschool and Primary Scale of Intelligence-III (WPPSI): The WPPSI is used to assess the cognitive abilities of children 2.6–7.3 years of age.

    The Differential Abilities Scales (DAS)—The DAS has two forms—Preschool version (age range 2.6–5.11) and the School Age version. (ages 6–17.11). The DAS provides 3 major Cluster Scores that tap Verbal, Spatial and Nonverbal abilities. DAS test results can be viewed from several different theoretical perspectives. The Nonverbal Cluster can be used with students who have language or hearing barriers.

    Cognitive Assessment System (CAS)—The CAS is based on the Luria Model of information processing and cognitive-neuropsychological theory (PASS). The PASS model stands for Planning, Attention, Simultaneous and Sequential processing. There is no verbal portion on this test and it is claimed to be more culturally fair than other tests which rely on learned academic skills.

    Stanford-Binet-V—The earliest version of this test is considered the first widely used cognitive assessment in America. The latest version has an extended age range from 2–85. The major domains included in this cognitive assessment are Fluid Reasoning, Knowledge, Quantitative Reasoning, Visual-Spatial and Working Memory.

Universal Nonverbal Intelligence Test (UNIT)—The UNIT is a good choice to use when assessing hearing-impaired or non-English speaking students. Major domains tested include complex memory, verbally mediated reasoning and nonverbal problem solving. The age range for this test is 5-17.11.

II. Intervention and Prevention

1. Know the different types of major counseling theories. Many of these theories are presented clearly in undergraduate introductory psychology texts.

2. Person-centered counseling—Strives for congruence between the real and ideal self. Its aim is to actualize a person's full potential and increase trust in oneself. Another major tenet of this theory is the belief that people naturally seek growth toward personal and universal goals. See concepts related to Abraham Maslow, Alfred Adler and Carl Rogers.

3. Existential counseling—Helps people find their unique meaning and purpose in the world. This type of counseling increases self-awareness and stresses the importance of "choice" in tough situations. The focus is on the present and future. See Victor Frankl's work.

4. Adlerian therapy—People are motivated by social interests and by striving toward goals. Life goals drive behavior. This method emphasizes taking a person's perspective and then altering it to yield productive results.

5. Psychoanalytic counseling—Freud's theory based on early life experiences of an individual. Unconscious motives and conflicts drive behavior. The goal of this method is to make one aware of his/her unconscious desires through interpretations. Be familiar with different Freudian stages, but most likely you do not have to memorize them. It appears that NASP is not too concerned with Freudian techniques. Rather emphasis is placed on Freud's general contributions to the field of psychology.

6. Systems Therapy—Individuals are part of a larger living system. Treatment of the entire family and various other systems is important in the therapeutic change process. This is also known as the ecological approach and seems to be a NASP endorsed perspective.

7. Cognitive-Behavioral Therapy (CBT)—This intervention approach is highly regarded and endorsed as best practice. Be familiar with many of its central principles. The C-B approach places an emphasis on a person's belief system as the cause of many problems. Internal dialogue plays a key role in behavior. Faulty assumptions and misconceptions must be addressed through talk and then modified through role-play or other active interventions.

8. Rational-Emotive counseling—Emphasizes confrontational techniques regarding irrational beliefs. See the work of Albert Ellis.

9. Gestalt therapy—Focuses on the wholeness and integration of thoughts, feelings and actions. In this therapy type, it is key to move a person from an external locus of control to an internal locus of control.

10. Reality therapy—Centers on choices people make and how they are working for them. (Dr. Phil seems to use this method because he always asks his clients, "How's that working for you?"). The objective is to have clients take charge of their own life by examining choices. See William Glasser's work.

11. Social Skills Training—Typically involves four processes: Instruction, rehearsing, providing feedback/reinforcement and reducing negative behaviors. Modeling and role-playing are important techniques in this intervention.

12. Response cost is an effective behavioral modification method. Response cost is the removal of an earned reward that usually reduces or modifies negative behaviors. For example, a student who throws food in the cafeteria must forgo his/her recess by cleaning up his/her mess. If the student is required to clean not only his/her food, but also must help clean the entire area, this is called "overcorrection." Overcorrection is a key piece in another technique called restorative justice.

13. Self-dialogue (self-talk) is a cognitive approach to changing behavior. It is vital to understand what a student is saying to himself or herself before, during and after an undesirable act. Changing self-talk can modify certain behaviors.

14. Know how to perform a Functional Behavioral Analysis (FBA). Remember the ABC's—Antecedence of the behavior, the Behavior itself and the Consequence (what maintains) the behavior.

15. Several school psychologists believe that all behavior is purposeful and is initiated by its antecedent (triggering event) and maintained by its consequences. Good interventionists always ask, "What is the payoff for the behavior?" If you change the trigger and the payoff for the target behavior, then the behavior will change.

16. In regards to behavioristic theory, know the differences between the various reinforcement schedules. The schedules are Fixed Ratio, Variable Ratio, Fixed Interval and Variable Interval. Of these schedules of reinforcement, Variable Interval shows the most resistance to change once the behavior is shaped by this method.

17. Know the differences between punishment, negative reinforcement and positive reinforcement. Remember that both negative and positive reinforcement increase behaviors, while punishment decreases behavior.

18. Behaviorists use the Premack principle to modify behavior. This principle emphasizes that a desirable task can reinforce a lower level task. For example, a child can eat a cookie (higher level task) after he/she finishes homework (lower level task).

19. A general counseling format that is commonly used in schools:

    1. Define the problem

    2. Brainstorm ideas to address the problem

    3. Implement the plan or modification

    4. Evaluate the intervention's effectiveness.

20. The key pieces for behavioral interventions are providing supportive feedback, giving choices to the student and supplying positive reinforcement.

III. General Psychological Concepts (Statistical and General Theories of Behavior)

A. Testing and Psychometric Concepts

1. Standard Deviation—Technically it is the square root of the variance. Deviation scores reflect differences and deviations from the Average (Mean). Plus/minus1 Standard Deviation holds roughly 68% of a given population. See the appendix for an illustration of the Bell Curve and Standard Deviation.

2. Most common cognitive assessments have a Mean (Average) of 100 and a Standard Deviation of 15 points. Therefore, if a student scores 118 on a cognitive test, that student is said to be slightly *over* 1 Standard Deviation above the Mean (above Average).

3. On the NASP test, watch for tricky questions regarding Standard Deviations. Remember that a Standard Score of 100 is Average, not 50. A Standard Score of 50 is considerably far below Average. However, a score that is in the 50th percentile (not percentage) is equal to a Standard Score of 100.

4. Some tests such as the old Stanford Binet have a Mean of 100 and a Deviation of 16 points. Be familiar with any differences between scores on various tests. Some questions might ask you to compare scores, so understand how to interpret Standard Scores.

5. Ipsative Scores—Examines a pattern of scores within an individual to determine relative (to self) strengths and weakness. Compares scores on a test to the test taker rather than to a group.

6. Criterion Measurement—This type of measurement is not based on the Bell Curve (Normal curve) population or group, but is based on a specific criteria or content to be mastered. Criterion measurement is used in self-paced studies.

7. Standard Error of Measurement (SEM)—is used to develop confidence brackets (intervals, or bandwidths) around a score on a standardized test. SEM represents the level of error expected in measuring a trait and a psychologist's confidence that a person's true score falls within a range of scores. For example, given a SEM of 5 points and a person scoring a 102 on a test, it can be said that person's true score falls within the range of 97 and 107 (subtract 5 and add 5 to the 102 score).

8. Z-scores—Mean of 0 and a SD of 1.

9. T-score—Mean of 50 and a SD of 10. A T-score of 65 would be above Average and 1.5 Standard Deviations above the Mean. Do not confuse T-scores with Standard Score.

10. Percentile—Percentage of people who score at or below the percentile score given on a test. Percentiles use percentages but are not percentages themselves.

11. Be aware of the key differences between types of scores. The reason professionals prefer to use Standard Scores is because they are "equal interval" scores, whereas other types of scores are not equal in their measurements of central tendency.

12. Effect size—A statistic that illustrates the overall effect of an intervention.

13. Standardized testing—Follows <u>strict</u> rules for administration, scoring and interpretation. Such tests have verifiable statistical properties associated with the test's validity and reliability. The chief benefit of standardized tests is that it compares a person to what is expected of a large population and shows what is "Normal".

14. Reliability—Is a vital characteristic for standardized tests. Reliability is the ability of a test to produce similar results over time. IQ test results remain somewhat stable (reliable) across time.

15. Validity—Another highly important test characteristic. Validity is a test's ability to measure what it purports to measure. For example, a reading test measures the ability to read, not to solve math problems.

16. Be familiar with the different types of validity such as predictive, convergent, discriminative and divergent validity. Typically, common standardized tests use convergent validity to support their use. An example of convergent validity is when a new test is correlated with an established test. If the new test has validity, it should have a high correlation with the older test.

17. Type I and II errors—Type I error is when you say something is true but it is not (rejecting a Null hypothesis). Type II is stating something is false, but it is really true (accepting a Null hypothesis).

18. Correlation—Is an association or relationship between variables. For example, research has shown a high correlation between smoking and lung cancer. However, remember that a strong correlation does not mean one variable *causes* another variable to change. Correlations above .70 are said to be strong and desirable for test purposes. Correlations are useful in predicting events. For example, IQ tests are useful in predicting a student's future grades. This is why when a child has a high IQ, but low achievement (grades), it is believed that something is interfering with that child's learning (such a learning disability).

19. Meta-analysis—Examines several studies to ascertain the validity of a construct or hypothesis. Generally speaking, meta-analytical studies are very powerful and persuasive in their findings.

20. To raise the "power" of an experiment, you must increase the number and types of participants. Raising the power makes your experiment's results more reliable and valid.

B. General Psychological Theories and Principles

1. Learned helplessness—A sense of hopelessness and depression that develops from a pattern of failures. See Martin Seligman's work with dogs.

2. Attribution theory—Carol Dweck's work on how people attribute success or failures to internal or external forces.

3. External locus of control is the belief that events happen to you. Success is attributed to "luck." Internal locus of control is the belief that one's effort and skills control one's future.

4. Behaviorism—focuses on the environment reinforcing behaviors. Behavioristic interventions and experiments are empirically driven and focus on strict data collection for scientific proof of effectiveness.

5. Social learning theory—This theory states that people learn not only through reinforcers and punishers (i.e. B.F. Skinner's Behaviorism) but also through observation. Albert Bandura illustrated that children can act aggressively by merely watching the violent behavior of others. The keyword to remember for Bandura's research is "modeling".

6. Be familiar with Kohlberg's stages of moral development. (1) The Pre-conventional stage is usually for children in which behavior is motivated by avoidance of punishments. (2) The Conventional stage is where most people are situated. The Conventional stage focuses on conformity of social norms and strives to avoid disapproval of others. (3) The Post-conventional stage centers on high ethics and moral principles of conscience (personal principles, not just laws of society).

7. Be familiar with Piaget's theories. Human development is the progressive adaptation to the environment through assimilation and

accommodation. Infants are biologically predisposed to develop and acquire information by interacting with their environment.

8.   According to Piaget, "accommodation" is the modification of mental schemes in response to the demands of the environment. For example, a child who thinks a dime is worth less than a nickel because it is physically smaller soon learns through play spending that it is actually worth more.

9.   According to Piaget, "assimilation" refers to using existing ideas in new situations—an attempt to generalize what is learned. For example, little Johnny uses a play hammer to hit his plastic blocks into holes. When he is given a large play wrench, he begins to hit the blocks the same way he did with his hammer.

10. Piaget's stages—

Sensorimotor (0–2 years old). Object permanence, attachment, little language and the child lives in the world of here and now.

Pre-operational (2–7 years) Covers K-1 grades. Egocentric, reason dominated by perception, intuitive rather than logical reasoning, does not fully understand that a short wide glass can hold more water than a tall thin glass (conservation).

Concrete stage (7–11 years) covers 2–6 grades. Ability to understand conservation, understands inferential thinking, quantitative reasoning, develops reversibility of thought ($5x2=10$ also means that $2x5 =10$).

Formal Operations (12–adult). This stage covers middle school and high school students. Students in this stage can deal with hypothetical situations and generalize learning. More adult-like in reasoning.

11. Be familiar with Erik Erikson's psychosocial stages—

Trust v. Mistrust (0–18 mos.) Attachment to caregiver is important at this stage. Develop sufficient trust with caregiver to explore world. Mother/father needs to be warm, loving and attentive to basic needs.

Autonomy v. Shame and Doubt (18 mos-3 years) Children start to develop a sense of confidence in their abilities to explore and to do things for themselves. Children begin to understand that they can control their behavior.

Initiative v. Guilt (3–5 years) Children move from simple self-control, as in the previous stage, to taking initiative in play and in various tasks. Imaginary play and choosing activities are illustrated at this stage.

Industry v. Inferiority (6–12 years). This stage covers the elementary school years, so know it well. Success or failure in school has lasting effect on self-efficacy and sense of adequacy. Children learn a sense of industry if they are recognized for various activities (painting, reading).

Identity v. Role Confusion (13–18 years) This stage covers the middle school and high school students. People develop a sense of identity, sense of self and strong ego during this time. Peers, role models and social pressure are factors associated with this stage.

The last few stages covered are important to review. However the age ranges covered by these stages typically fall beyond the target population of school psychologists. The other stages are—**Intimacy v. Isolation, Generativity v. Stagnation (or selfishness); and Integrity v. Despair.**

12. Freudian or psychoanalytic theory may be on some NASP tests, but my research has not revealed that this area is the basis for more than just one or two questions. It seems Freud's contributions to school psychology are broad in nature. Instead of memorizing his stages of development, I would be familiar with the Freudian concepts that are not controversial and are practical in nature. For example, Freud was one of the first psychologists to realize the importance of "critical periods" and the significance of early experiences. Be familiar with how the id, ego and superego interact.

13. Review developmental disabilities typically associated with Special Education. Be able to recognize hallmark traits for various disabilities. For example, know the traits associated with Autism (PDD), Asperger's Syndrome, Fragile X, Down Syndrome, Mental Retardation, Bi-polar Disorder and Attention Deficit Hyperactivity Disorder.

14. Autism impacts more males than females and is a relatively low incidence disorder. Prevalence rates for Autism spectrum disorders range from 1 in every 2,500 people to 1-10,000, but this figure may change due to recent advances in diagnosing the disorder. Behavior modification, "shaping" and direct hands-on teaching with pictures are common interventions for children with Autism. Also, the use of

toys, increased structure, motor imitation and family participation are useful methods to use. Currently, there is no cure for Autism.

15. Down Syndrome (Trisomy 21) impacts 1 out of 800 people. The disorder is believed to be caused by an extra chromosome (chromosomal disorder). Most children with this disorder also have mental retardation. Interventions associated with this disorder include hands-on learning, tight structure in the classroom, visual communication systems and social skills training. There is no cure for Down Syndrome.

16. Tourettes—This is a tic disorder with a genetic component. Relaxation, social skills training, medication and cognitive-behavioral interventions are widely utilized with this disorder. This disorder may involve involuntary twitching, facial expression or verbal outbursts. Tics may become more apparent after the use of stimulant medication to treat a co-occurring problem like ADHD.

17. Mental Retardation Standard IQ test scores given a Standard Deviation of 15 points: SS=55-69 is considered mild retardation, SS=40-54 is moderate and below 40 is severe.

18. SLIC—This acronym stands for Significant Limited Intellectual Capacity. Children who are SLIC must have Standard IQ scores at least 2 Standard Deviations below the mean (Standard Scores less than 70) *and* adaptive skills as measures by standardized surveys also below 70.

19. SIED—Stands for Significant Identifiable Emotional Disability. The key to this disability is that children must be impacted in various settings and one setting must be at school. Emotional disturbances cannot be due to situational factors and interventions must have been attempted.

20. Speech and Language Disabilities—Children with this disability have difficulty with expressive and/or receptive language. Either part must fall below the 9th percentile on a speech language assessment such as the CELF or Peabody tests.

21. ESL—stands for English as a Second Language. Foreign students are typically placed in ESL classes in schools because they do not fully understand the English language. It seems NASP desires ESL students be provided education in both languages. Full immersion or

instruction only within a child's native language is generally not supported.

22. Readiness—This term is used to denote a student's biological and physiological maturational level to enter school (usually kindergarten).

23. Attention Deficit Hyperactivity Disorder (ADHD) is considered one of the most prevalent disorders seen in schools and usually co-occurs with other problems such as learning disabilities. In large schools, typically 3–7% of the population will be diagnosed with ADHD. The disorder impacts boys more than girls with a 3:1 ratio commonly cited. Hallmark traits of ADHD could include impulsivity, inability to sustain attention, constant movement and lack of self-regulation.

IV. Educational Principles and Methods

1. This area may cover consultation with teachers regarding teaching strategies and classroom management techniques. Be familiar with various consultation models. An essential idea to keep in mind is that NASP seems to endorse the "indirect" service model, which seeks to build up the consultee's skills (teacher's skills). If you have questions on the NASP exam regarding the most effective model, it is probably the indirect service model. Read Gerald Caplan's work on Consultation Models.

2. Client Centered Consultation—Benefits only one client (student). Example, when a teacher has a problem with a student, the school psychologist intervenes with the student. This method can produce desired results, but it is time consuming. Generally speaking, it is best practice to teach teachers how to help themselves.

3. Consultee Centered—This consultation model benefits the teacher by building his/her skills that might be used to help numerous other people. In other words, the psychologist helps the teacher develop new skills to support his/her students. This model seems to be best practice at the present time.

4. Program Centered Administrative Consultation—Benefits an entire program or school. For example, a school psychologist performs an in-service for a school.

5. Consultee-Centered Administrative Model—A school psychologist teaches skills to other key administrators to effect change at many schools or a district.

6. A common "problem solving" consultation format:

    1. Define the problem—be specific.

    2. Analyze the problem and collect data if necessary.

    3. Plan an intervention-monitor and modify as necessary

    4. Evaluate your outcome and compare pre-post data.

7. Other consultation models—Ecological (Systems) Model examines how a person's behavior is being maintained within various settings and systems. The Process Consultation model uses workgroups, feedback and work co-ordinations between groups.

8. Examples of effective classroom management methods:

    A. Classroom rules are explicitly stated and posted in the room.

    B. Seating arrangements (desk arrangements, students sitting by friends) can impact the flow and order of the class.

    C. Rules must be consistently and immediately enforced. Consistency is essential in most classroom management strategies.

    D. Teachers must give feedback to the students.
    Meaningful performance feedback is vital and must be consistently given. Feedback is effective if it is precise and instructive rather than punitive.

    E. Point and level systems are effective if they are _easy_ to implement.

    F. Structure and predictable routines are very important to students.

    G. Preserve the dignity of all students. Teachers should not shame students or engage in power struggles. The teacher is the adult leader that students look to for structure and expectations. If rules are broken, teachers should give students choices to amend their behavior. If the student's choice is poor, or if the behavior continues, then the teacher simply implements "natural consequences" without undue attention or argument.

H. When giving a directive, teachers should stand in close proximity to the student. Proximity is an important classroom management practice.

I. If rewards or punishments are used, they must be given promptly after the undesirable behavior. Additionally, rewards must be salient (valued by the person) to be effective.

9. It is best practice to involve parents when a student presents a concern or problem. Always document the time and type of parent contact.

10. NASP endorses parental notification and involvement. Typically, teachers are encouraged to involve parents when a student is having academic or behavioral concerns. On the exam, usually any response option that involves parental contact has a high probability of being the correct answer.

11. Understand the differences between phonics instruction and whole language instruction. Generally, the sounding of letters to form words (phonics) is an effective instructional method for young students.

12. Children with phonemic awareness have a good foundation to start reading. Phonemic awareness is the ability to hear, segment and manipulate word sounds. For example, a typical phonemic awareness screener asks a student to say a word, "play" and to say it again without a certain sound like the "p" sound. The answer would be "lay."

13. NASP endorses the use of positive reinforcement in the classroom. There is a strong movement to support and use a child's strengths as much as possible. This is called a "capacity" model.

14. Token economies, while using positive reinforcers, are criticized as not being practical because they are cumbersome to implement by teachers. Token economies or reward systems are useful if they are easy and practical to maintain.

15. A teaching method that encourages breaking a complex task into smaller tasks is widely acceptable practice.

16. Teachers should be encouraged to make learning meaningful to students by explicitly showing them how a lesson is beneficial to their lives, or important to society. Students want to understand "why" they have to learn certain concepts.

17. Many times, effective teachers briefly review with their students the previous day's learning and will explicitly preview the parts of a new assignment before each class. Sometimes the schedule for new learning is written on the board for all to see (a visual component is important).

18. Teachers are encouraged to use a multisensory approach. It is best practice to use auditory, visual and tactile methods when teaching. Teachers in middle school and high school sometimes need to be reminded of the many different types of learners. It is interesting that high school lectures appeal mostly to auditory learners.

19. Know the differences between the terms "accommodation" and "modification" as it relates to special education services. Accommodations refer to changes in the environment, such as letting a student use a quiet room to take a test. A modification is actually changing a task to perform. For example, a student who has difficulty with writing might be allowed to complete half the number of questions than his/her peers.

20. The ultimate goal and role of special education services is to increase students' level of independence and responsibility.

21. Review Curriculum Based Assessment (CBA) and Curriculum Based Measurement (CBM) for the NASP exam. CBA is used in program evaluations, while CBM is commonly utilized for classroom/instructional intervention planning.

22. According to cognitive-behavioral theorists, learning is supported by mental representations of new concepts with existing concepts (schema) and through associations (the pairing of a skill or idea with a reinforcer).

V. Legal and Ethical Considerations

1. In most professions, the ethical and legal sections of a licensure test are regarded as the most challenging. The reason for this is that such questions are usually higher up on Bloom's taxonomy and require the examinees to "apply" their knowledge rather than recite facts. Be highly familiar with landmark legal cases and the laws specifically governing education. It may not be necessary to memorize all of the case laws, but be able to recognize and understand the impact of most prominent legal cases.

2. As mentioned earlier, NASP seems to endorse the notion of getting parental notification and parental involvement. The same holds true for any type of school board question—community involvement is best

practice. Therefore, answer relevant test questions that have a positive parental involvement choice.

3. Study the Individuals with Disabilities Education Act (IDEA—Public Law 94-142) very thoroughly. Note the changes in the IDEA act because it is modified (re-authorized by Congress) periodically. The IDEA act gives the right to a free and appropriate public education in the least restrictive environment (LRE) for all students.

4. FERPA—Family Education Right to Privacy Act. This act was sponsored in 1974 and is sometimes called the Buckley Amendment. This act gives families the right to review the records of their child and the files must be kept confidential. The public and people that do not have legal privileges cannot review a student's file. Confidentiality is central to this law.

5. Section 504. This is a Civil Rights law and guarantees access to a school building and to a school's curriculum. Many people mistakenly believe this is an educational law, but it is important to remember the Office of Civil Rights, not the Department of Education, enforces it. Section 504 is a law governing the rights of handicapped people. Students with hearing or vision problems sometimes fall under this law. Also, in some cases, children with ADHD are said to have a physical handicap and therefore are entitled to have full access to the general curriculum.

6. Brown v. Board of Education—Educational facilities are not allowed to segregate according to race (Anti-segregation law).

7. Hobson v. Hansen—Schools must provide equal educational opportunities despite a family's socio-economic status (SES). Review laws regarding "ability" tracking.

8. Diana v. State Board of Education—Assessments must be administered in the native languages of the students (must be able to validate minority testing practices). This is similar to another case—Guadalupe v. Temple School District. In this case, it was ruled that students cannot be identified as mentally retarded unless they were properly assessed by considering the student's primary language and had scores at least 2 Standard Deviations below the mean.

9. Larry P v. Riles—This landmark case in California ruled that the percentage of minority students placed in special education classrooms couldn't exceed the percentage in the representative population. This ruling was based on the fact that there was an over-representation of minorities classified as mentally retarded.

10. PASE v. Hannon—This is a pro-special education ruling that endorsed the use of standardized tests as long as they are not culturally biased and are used with several other measures.

11. Marshall v. Georgia—This case is also a pro-special education ruling that stood in contrast to the Larry P. case. The Marshall ruling stated that the percentage of minorities placed in special education can exceed the percentage in the representative population as long as the appropriate and proper steps for placement were followed.

12. Honig v. Doe—Special education students must have a manifestation hearing to review placement if they are suspended more than ten days.

13. Gifted education—At this point in time, federal law does not require services or funding for those students who are gifted (IQ> 130). However, the reader should research this area of law to ascertain whether laws are different in individual states.

14. Rowley v. Board of Education—This is an important landmark case wherein the judge stated public schools do not have to provide the best education, but an adequate education. In other words, schools do not have to provide a Cadillac, but a Ford. (Hint: never say the previous statement to a parent).

15. Tarasoff Case—This is a well-known case that is an interesting story. In short, the court ruled that a school district has a duty to warn the parents if their son/daughter is in danger (Important for anti-bullying programs).

16. Lau v. Nichols Case—Schools must provide accommodations for ESL students.

17. IDEA law of 1997, Part "C," authorized Child Find for children 0–3 years old. This law was based on PL-94-457, Education of the Handicapped Act. PL-94-457 authorized early intervention of toddlers and families.

18. Perkins Act—Gives rights to transition special educational students into vocational programs. Occupational access.

19. Be familiar with the No Child Left Behind Act (NCLB) and how it impacts school districts. A notable feature of this law is that it requires schools to employ "highly" qualified staff and has high standards that are gauged by objective measures. Schools that do not meet NCLB standards are at risk for losing federal money and support.

Special Content Areas: Neuropsychology, Crisis Intervention and TBI.

This is an additional section because its content did not fit neatly under the five major areas noted in chapter one. Moreover, these three topics are relatively new and have emerging research associated with them. It is my opinion that these areas, despite their newcomer status, will have a tremendous impact on the field of school psychology. Recent graduates in school psychology might have a slight knowledge advantage over veteran school psychologists within these areas because 5 years ago relevant course work was not even required. Neuropsychological research is especially dynamic, and advances within this field change from year to year.

Do not expect many questions on the NASP exam regarding these areas. You might only have two or three questions. However, future NASP tests will likely have more questions related to these topics because of their recognized importance.

Neuropsychology (Also See Appendix)

1. There are four major lobes of the brain that play a major role in processing information and regulating behavior.

    Frontal Lobes—Responsible for "executive functions." This area does not necessarily processes information as much as it controls other aspects of the brain (the brain manager or executive). This lobe helps in planning future actions and regulates behavior. It is also responsible for cognitive flexibility and helps people "shift" to different aspects of problem solving or topics.

    Parietal Lobes—Located roughly on the top portion of the brain. This area helps to assimilate body sensations. It also helps with developing symbolic associations and math skills. Sometimes this area integrates information.

    Temporal lobe—Located near and under the ears, this area of the brain processes auditory information and is implicated in reading problems (phonemic awareness difficulties).

    Occipital Lobe—Located at the back of the head, this area is responsible for processing visual information.

2. While there are areas of the brain (lobes) that are primarily responsible for specific functions, the brain works as a "whole" unit and needs all parts to work together.

3. The area of memory is still being researched and there are no definitive answers when it comes to memory. It appears that no one particular area

is responsible for storing all memories, but is diffused throughout the brain. A major part of the brain called the hippocampus is implicated in *forming* memories because of its role in associating emotions with events.

4.   The amygdala is associated with emotions and emotional responses.

5.   ADHD is associated with a dysfunction within the frontal lobes. However, ADHD research is still emerging. Reference, Dr. Russell Barkley' work.

6.   The cerebral cortex is associated with higher order reasoning.

7.   Broca's area and Wernicke's area are implicated in speech/language problems and reading difficulties.

8.   Aphasia is the inability to use language and Agnosia is the inability to identify seen objects.

9.   The left hemisphere of the brain is largely (but not totally) responsible for language, speaking, writing, math and coordinating some complex movements. The right hemisphere aids in recognizing patterns, faces, spatial relations and recognizing emotions.

10. The limbic system (part of the lower brain) houses those areas (amygdala, hippocampus and others) responsible for our emotions.

Traumatic Brain Injury (TBI)

1.   Traumatic brain injury is sometimes referred to as acquired brain injury—although both definitions are evolving and becoming more specific. TBI causes over 53,000 deaths a year and is a leading cause of death in children under 18 years old. Research in the area of head injury is advancing at a very fast pace and some new theories are contradicting theories from just a few years ago.

2.   Even mild concussions (blows to the head) can cause permanent damage or information processing dysfunctions (commonly associated with learning disabilities). Children may seem okay after a hit to the head, but damage and swelling may occur. Children with significant TBI require frequent assessments because they may show drastic changes in the first year of recovery. Both cognitive and personality changes could be evident.

3.   There is great debate over the "elasticity" (how the brain heals itself) of a child's brain. Current research illustrates that children are more at risk for permanent brain damage than adults. The younger the developmental age, the more at risk the person is for various types of long term problems. Age

of the TBI and type of TBI are extremely important for assessment and planning interventions.

4.   A hit to one part of the head can affect the entire brain, the immediate area of the brain, or the other side of the brain. The two types of blows (insults) are classified as "focal" (pointed) and "diffused."

5.   Cognitive tests can help determine the functioning of the brain (what the person can do) after a head trauma. IQ tests for older TBI victims typically show a large amount of variation between subtest scores. However, very young children sometimes show uniformly low subtest scores.

6.   Interventions for TBI victims should focus on what the child can do and build upon those strengths (capacity or strength-based approach).

Crisis Intervention

1.   Increasingly, school psychologists are called to be a vital part of a school's crisis interventions team. A crisis can be a bomb threat, intruder in the building, student suicide or natural disaster.

2.   Preparation and rehearsal is key to crisis response. Schools should have explicit crisis plans in place at the beginning of every school year. A "team" approach to crisis is best practice. Specific duties and roles should be spelled out before each school year.

3.   Community resources and links should be established at the beginning of the school year. In the eventuality of a school crisis, community resources should be readily accessible.

4.   Emergency phone trees should be handed out at the beginning of the year.

5.   Debriefing people involved in a crisis is a technique to relay information and a way to flag those people who may need more mental health support. Debriefing is not a therapeutic intervention per se, although it does have some therapeutic qualities.

6.   NASP has articles related to crisis interventions and the role of the school psychologist: check the NASP website for details. During and after a crisis, school psychologists should be highly visible and ready to link those in need with services.

7.   Be familiar with the symptoms and the treatment of Post Traumatic Stress Disorder (PTSD). PTSD is commonly associated with a crisis.

Stress symptoms may not evince themselves for days, months or years after the trauma. Symptoms in children may be masked behind inappropriate behaviors (fighting, bed wetting, withdrawal). Psychological treatment for PTSD is similar for anxiety disorders. It seems like a cognitive-behavioral (C-B) approach is effective if it utilizes self-calming techniques, positive visualizations and empathetic perspective taking.

8. Be familiar with how to perform a suicide assessment and how to handle related cases. For example, always detain a suspected suicidal student and notify parents (regardless of your assessment conclusions).

9. Know the differences between a primary, secondary and tertiary intervention. Remember that prevention is a primary intervention.

10. First responders to a crisis are at risk of suffering emotional difficulties. Crisis counselors may need support just as much as victims.

11. There is no specific profile of school "shooters," although some general traits may exists. Bullying seems to play a central role in making some students act violently.

12. An excellent resource that is easy to read is published by the United States Secret Service: *Threat Assessment in Schools: A Guide to Managing Threatening Situations and Creating Safe School Climates. May, 2002.*

CHAPTER THREE

A Practice Test

The following practice test does not contain the exact questions as the real test. However, several items, the fundamental structure, and the format are very similar to the actual NASP exam. It is important to remember that most exam questions tap constructs that have a myriad of ancillary facts associated with it. Therefore, the reader needs to fully understand all the related concepts each question addresses.

During this trial run, ask yourself several questions about the underlying concept of each item. You may even ask yourself how each test question could be asked differently. It is strongly recommended that you make notes regarding the questions you need to know more about. Notice the types of questions you miss the most. Are the missed questions the Legal/Ethical ones or the Assessment ones? Also, be familiar with keywords and how those keywords are usually found in the correct response choice.

The benefit of taking practice tests is that it is an excellent way to study for the real test. Practice testing hones your skills such as time management and response selection. It also decreases your anxiety because it takes some of the mystery out of the real exam. After this trial exam, it might be beneficial to take two or three shorter one-hour tests. Ask your study group to help design these brief mock exams.

Ready yourself as you would in an *actual testing situation*. Treat the following practice test as the real test. Turn the page, read the directions carefully and begin!

Directions: You have *two hours* to complete the following test. Be mindful to keep *strict* time limits. Mark the *best* answer by completely filling in the oval next to your choice. Sometimes, two answers will be true, but mark the one that is *"most"* appropriate. Do not leave any questions blank. If you change your answer, erase your previous choice thoroughly. (Advice: Put a small check on those questions that are very difficult to answer and move on to the next item. Remember to go back to the marked questions and complete them after finishing the test.)

Answers are provided in the back of the guide.

Ready? Good Luck.   Start Timing: 120 minutes

1.   Sue is a second grade student who struggles with reading. It happens that Sue's teacher lives next door to a reading specialist in the school district. Sue's teacher asked her neighbor to look at Sue's standardized reading test to offer some advice. What law has Sue's teacher violated?

O   The Federal Confidentiality Act of 1975

O   No law was violated because teachers are government employees

O   IDEA law right to privacy

O   Family Education and Right to Privacy Act (FERPA)

2.   Norm Chomsky is known for what psychological idea?

O   People have a predisposition to acquire language

O   Children who come from impoverished backgrounds are more likely to have behavioral and emotional difficulties.

O   Whole word reading is innate

O   Most male students are visual learners

3. A school board wants to adopt a new, but controversial math curriculum. As a school psychologist, you are called in for consultation. What do you tell the school board is best practice?

    O There will be resistance from some parents, but most parents are looking to the board for leadership so any decision must be final.

    O Concerned parents need a way to voice their concerns during the adoption phase.

    O The board needs to have an absolute consensus because everyone must agree on such an important issue.

    O The board needs to utilize curriculum experts to make informed decisions.

4. Which type of goal setting is most appropriate when teaching teenage students?

    O Moderate goal setting within the zone of proximal development

    O Mastery goal setting to decrease anxiety

    O Performance goal setting based on classroom norms.

    O High goals and standards keep students striving for achievement

5. Which brain chemical is largely implicated in depression?

    O melatonin

    O serotonin

    O neuropeptides

    O endorphines

6. You are asked to perform an emotional assessment on a child who is withdrawn. Your first thought is to check for depression. What is the most appropriate tool to use in your assessment?

    O The BASC

    O The Vineland

    O The Clinical Scales of Depression in Children

    O The Beck Depression Inventory

7. A child you recently assessed with the Differential Abilities Scales (DAS) had an overall Standard Score of 85. The student's Vineland survey from the teacher showed a Standard Score of 63 and the parent's Vineland resulted in a Standard Score of 87. You determine the discrepancy between the adaptive assessment scores is most likely due to?

    O Measurement error inherent in all tests

    O The child behaves differently in different settings

    O The subjectivity and different perceptions of raters

    O The difficulty associated with completing complex surveys

8. One of the most effective interventions for a child with ADHD is?

    O Placing him/her near the front of the classroom

    O Increasing the student's self-awareness and knowledge of the disorder

    O Having the student exercise before school to drain hyperactive energy

    O Consistently reminding the student to take his/her medication (Ritalin, Adderall)

9. A tenth grade teacher has a visually impaired student who is given an extensive assignment. In this case, how should the teacher proceed?

    O Allow other students to help the impaired student.

    O The teacher should set aside a special time to discuss optional modifications of the assignment with the student.

    O The visually impaired student should not be required to complete the entire assignment due to his/her handicapping condition.

    O The task should be assigned as a joint effort between the teacher's assistant and the visually impaired student.

10. You are given a new cognitive assessment for which you have no formal training to administer. The parents of a student you will be testing are strongly requesting that you give their son the new test. From what you have read and heard from colleagues, the new test is highly regarded. What should you do in this situation?

    O Ethically, you cannot administer the test and must use a more familiar test.

    O You should practice with the test and administer it with supervision.

O You need to refer the case to another colleague who has administered the test.

O Ask a colleague to give the test, but be present during the administration.

11. Your assistant principal notifies you that a seventh grade student has drawings depicting death. When asked why the student drew such things, she stated she thinks people who commit suicide are cool. After intervening and speaking with the student, what should you do next?

O notify the parents of this situation.

O Call the police and local suicide hotline for assistance.

O Notify social services and the school social worker.

O If the assessment shows the student is not in danger, make a note to the student's file and closely monitor the situation.

12. You just completed a comprehensive assessment that has taken several days. The student you tested has a low IQ score and is considered low functioning. The student wants to know about his performance and asks you to explain your results. What is best practice in this situation?

O Tell the student that the results tell you information on how he/she learns. The details should not be disclosed.

O Be truthful but brief with the student when you discuss the results.

O Secure permission from the parents before discussing assessment findings.

O Discuss the results with both the student and teacher at the same time.

13. You work in a school district where many parents use illegal drugs. You are concerned about one particular elementary school that you spend two days a week servicing. You have heard students talk about wanting to use drugs. What is an effective intervention in this case?

O Talk to individual classes about drug abuse.

O Start a school-wide anti-drug campaign.

O Teach teachers how to talk with students about drugs.

O Gather parental, school and community support to raise awareness and address the drug problem at school.

14. What memory technique should students use to remember long series of numbers?

O Chunking

O Write the numbers on paper

O Repeating the number series rapidly back to yourself.

O Teach students to look for number patterns to help them.

15. According to the information-processing model, incoming information is encoded into what first?

O Long-term memory (LTM)

O The temporal lobe of the brain

O Bits of information that are associated with conditional stimuli.

O Short term memory (STM)

16. Diane is a sophomore at a large public school. At the beginning of the year Diane felt bullied by Sally. The principal at that time quickly intervened and stopped the bullying. Now, at mid-year, Diane reports to the administration that Sally is once again making unpleasant comments. The principal this time suspends Sally for two days and calls Sally's parents. What else should you advise the principle do?

O Call Diane's parents to notify them of the situation.

O Make sure Diane has mental health support if needed.

O Have Diane talk with the school psychologist or social worker on how to deal effectively with harassment in the future.

O Have Sally sign a contract that outlines the terms of appropriate future behavior. The contract is necessary for re-admittance.

17. Your school district asks you review a new cognitive assessment. While reading the technical manual you notice that the one year test-retest reliability coefficient is .77. You also make a note that the new test was correlated with a well-known test to determine convergent validity. The convergent correlation coefficient for the two tests was .60. You can tell your district—

O The new test has acceptable reliability and validity.

O   The new test's reliability coefficient supports the idea that the test measures what it is designed to measure.

O   The correlation between the new and old test shows a modest association, but cannot be considered strong enough to recommend using the new test.

O   The new test should be utilized by the district.

18.   Metacognition refers to what?

O   Knowledge and self-awareness about one's own thoughts and abilities.

O   A useful reading technique.

O   A psychoanalytic counseling method used to help students think about their abilities and subsequent choices.

O   The ability to activate prior knowledge when trying to make a reading passage meaningful.

19-20. Seth is a 9th grade student with a SIED label. He has several clinical disorders including ADHD and bi-polar disorder. During the school day, Seth is able to control most of his behaviors, but not all. Despite his Above Average cognitive scores, his grades are not stellar. However, he is passing all classes with C's. Seth's teachers think he would benefit from more self-contained special education classes. What would you advise his teachers?

O   Tell his teachers to keep data to track Seth's progress. The data will be used during his next Annual Review IEP meeting to change his placement.

O   Tell the teachers that Seth's placement should be in the least restrictive environment and a more contained placement may not be warranted.

O   The special education team should discuss the issue with Seth's parents and then move him into more supportive classes once parental permission is secured.

O   Ask the parents what they want in this situation.

20.   Seth's parents are very upset that he is making mostly C's. Even though he is receiving special support services, his cognitive scores suggest that he should be making very high grades. The parents are threatening to file a

lawsuit if Seth is not assigned increased para-educator time to address his needs more thoroughly. What most likely will happen in this situation?

O The school is providing a "reasonable" education and does not have to supply all services. Therefore, the lawsuit will likely be unsuccessful.

O The high cost of going to court will most likely force the school district to grant the parents' wishes.

O The parents and school district know that an IEP is a legal document and once a child is receiving special services, he/she is entitled under federal law to be provided all services.

O The parents will have to go to arbitration before a lawsuit can be filed.

21. You have administered the Cognitive Assessment System (CAS) to evaluate a student's cognitive functioning. The student's overall (general) Standard Score is 50. How do you interpret this score?

O The student's performance is considered Average given the range of scores is 1-100.

O The student's score is roughly 2 Standard Deviations below Average.

O The student most likely has a significant learning disability.

O The student's performance falls within the mentally retarded range of Standardized Scores.

22. What is the approximate age range for the Wechsler Intelligence Test for Children Forth Edition (WISC-IV)?

O 5–16 years of age

O 3–16.5 years of age

O 5–17 years of age

O 6–16.11 years of age

23. Rational Emotive Therapy (RET) is founded upon what hypothesis?

O That people's difficulties and problems stem from the choices they make. To change behavior, a therapist examines the individual's clarity of thinking and faulty beliefs.

O A person's behavior is maintained by consequences.

O Behavior is embedded in a dynamic environment. To change behavior, one must considered the individual's family, peer relations and emotional needs.

O Behavior is driven by unconscious drives to ease anxiety and to be accepted unconditionally by peers.

24. School "readiness" is related to which of the following?

O A condition that exists when maturation is sufficiently developed to allow the rapid acquisition of basic academic skills.

O When a child is able to control his/her behavior, he/she can attend school.

O This is a term used to illustrate that a student is ready to advance to the next grade level.

O A student is considered in a state of "readiness" when he/she is focused and attending to auditory and visual information.

25. On a cognitive assessment, a student has a Verbal and Performance split of 15 points. The Full Scale score is a Standard Score of 95. How would you interpret the student's assessment if he/she had a suspected reading problem noted by his/her teacher?

O The split between V and P is significant, but not necessarily clinical.

O It can be safely stated that the child has a learning disability.

O The Full Scale score is invalid and cannot be used.

O It is considered best practice to administer a different cognitive test due to the difficulty interpreting scores with such variations.

26. How does SOMPA view standardized cognitive testing?

O Some children are late bloomers and therefore IQ tests are not reliable for children under 6 years of age.

O SOMPA assumes that a child's cultural background can mask his/her true potential which is not illustrated on many IQ tests.

O SOMPA is an organization that advocates for the rights of minority populations that are over-represented in special education classrooms.

O SOMPA supports the use of standardized tests that are objectively shown to demonstrate statistical reliability and validity.

27. In a reading group, which type of person is likely to emerge as the leader of the group?

   O The attractive person

   O The social person

   O The smartest person

   O The comedian

28. Curriculum based measurements (CBM) are used for what purposes?

   O CBM measures a school's progress toward explicit academic standards.

   O CBM is especially effective when used to evaluate a teacher's skills.

   O Measures a sample of a student's work over time to determine if an instructional method is effective.

   O CBM is a measurement and assessment method that will most likely supplant standardized testing because it is considered an "authentic" tool.

29. Which brain structure is usually associated with emotions?

   O Parietal lobe

   O Broca's area

   O Left frontal gyrus

   O Amygdala

30. You are treating a student who is shy and unassertive. What is the most effective therapeutic approach in this case?

   O Rational Emotive Therapy (RET)

   O Person Centered (Rogerian) Therapy

   O Cognitive-Behavioral therapy that uses modeling and rehearsal

   O Behavior Therapy that rewards assertive behaviors

31. A school psychologist's duties are not solely devoted to special education students. When you are asked to counsel and/or assess the emotional state of a student by a teacher or parent, it is best practice to do what first?

O Although a student may not be danger to him/herself or others, a school psychologist should always meet with any student who needs counseling.

O A psychologist should secure written permission from the parents to perform therapeutic and diagnostic services.

O Although important, it is not mandatory to secure permission to meet with students because such services are free to all public school students.

O School psychologists have a license or certificate from the state in which they work. Therefore, a psychologist can counsel students because it falls within the scope of their licensed duties.

32. You are asked to consult with a teacher regarding a classroom management problem. What is the best approach?

O A non-hierarchal collaborative model should be followed.

O A client-centered model is usually most effective.

O A cognitive-behavioral consultation model typically produces effective results.

O The ecological model is the most modern approach in this case.

33. Jack is a second grade student who struggled academically last year. He is not a behavioral problem and is somewhat reticent in class. At the end of the current school year, the parents are thinking that Jack should repeat the second grade because his grades are still very low. How would you advise Jack's parents?

O Interventions should be tried first and their effectiveness documented. Retention is typically not an effective strategy.

O Jack, his parents and teachers should be given the *Light's Standardized Retention Scales* to help determine if he should be retained.

O Talk with Jack's parents and teachers about assessing him for special education services.

O Jack's parents should be told that retaining a student, while very difficult for the parents, is usually an effective means of helping the student in the long term.

34. Which cognitive assessment is best suited for deaf students or students who do not speak English?

    O The Differential Abilities Scales (DAS)-Nonverbal

    O The WISC-IV with an interpreter

    O The Universal Nonverbal Intelligence Test (UNIT)

    O The Cognitive Assessment System (CAS)

35. For what disorder is flooding or in vivo therapy associated?

    O Phobias and anxiety

    O Depression and withdrawal

    O Bi-polar disorder

    O Attention Deficit Disorder

36. According to Erikson, children in second grade are negotiating which stage of development?

    O Initiative versus guilt

    O Industry versus inferiority

    O Peer pressure to conform

    O attachment to teachers and respect for authority

37. When implementing a crisis intervention for an off-campus suicide, the second step is to?

    O Dedicate a memorial

    O Speak to classes of the deceased student.

    O Have a school assembly

    O Plan to have a brief service at school to show respect for the deceased student.

38. NASP recommends that school psychologist should directly supervise no more than how many interns at one time?

    O 2

    O 3

O 4

O 8

39. Which law requires that all children be identified for special services by school districts?

   O Section 504 of the civil rights law

   O Free and Appropriate Education Act of 1977

   O Individuals with Disabilities Education Act (IDEA)

   O The Hohnbaum Amendment

40. Which of the following is considered the first IQ test made for children?

   O The WISC-I

   O The Standford-Binet

   O The Bellevue Test

   O The Scholastic Aptitude Test—Alpha Series

41. The use of projective tests (Rorschach, Draw a Person) is usually used for?

   O Building rapport with a student.

   O Gathering supplementary information about a student.

   O Determining if a student is prone to malingering and deception.

   O These tests should never be used in schools due to poor reliability.

42. Parental complaints regarding Section 504 should be directed to which area?

   O The Department of Education

   O The school district's administration office

   O The Office of Civil Rights

   O The State's Board of Education

43. What is the primary difference between achievement tests and cognitive tests?

   O IQ tests are norm referenced

   O Achievement tests are generally broader in content than IQ tests

O Cognitive tests (IQ) are typically used to predict future learning more than achievement tests.

O Cognitive tests use Standard Scores, while achievement tests use grade-equivalent scores.

44. You find out that another school psychologist has violated an ethical rule. What should you do first?

O Attempt to talk with the person directly and address the situation informally.

O Immediately report the situation to school officials because you have an ethical obligation to do so.

O Notify the school psychologist that if he/she does not report the violation, you will have to report it.

O Not all ethical violations are legal violations. Usually, you do not have to take any action.

45-46. A student was referred to you due to his behavioral disruptions in class. After a series of interventions, the special education team and parents agree that formal assessments should be initiated. The results from your formal cognitive assessment demonstrated that the student has a very large verbal and nonverbal difference between scores. Other streams of information support the contention that the student has a learning disability—specifically a nonverbal learning disability.

45. The parents have difficulty accepting your findings and demand to see the test protocol. Your response should be?

O Show the protocol to the parents and give them a copy if they request it.

O Refuse to let the parents examine the protocol citing copyright laws and the need to keep testing material strictly confidential.

O Provide the parents with qualitative information and your reasoning when interpreting the test results. The protocol may be used in your explanation, but not copied.

O Reiterate for the parents that the identification of a learning disability is a team decision and multiple pieces of information were used in the determination. After your explanation, supply the parents with all the necessary scores.

46. After a lengthy explanation, the parents in the above example are still refuting your results and want outside (private) testing done. Which of the following statements is most true?

    O The parents can have a private assessment done at the school district's expense if they complete the formal appeals process.

    O Parent's can have a private assessment, but the school district is not obligated to pay for outside testing.

    O Private assessments are never paid for by a public school district.

    O Only a judge can order private testing that is paid for by a school district.

47. A high school student is in your office requesting to see you. He is visibly and extremely upset because of a serious fight he had with his girlfriend last night. You do not have permission to counsel him. What is "best practice" in this situation?

    O You are not allowed to counsel a student without parent permission.

    O It is acceptable to perform a brief intervention in emergency or crisis situations.

    O Refer the student to his counselor at school.

    O Have the student wait in a supervised room until his parents can be contacted.

48. At what point in a counseling relationship do you explain the limitations of confidentiality?

    O During your initial meeting.

    O After a solid rapport has been established.

    O When your sessions with the student are nearing completion.

    O If the student asks what will be disclosed to his/her parents.

49. A parent and teacher complete an adaptive scales survey (Vineland) on a child suspected of having a cognitive impairment. The parent's version is significantly different than that of the teacher's version, what do you do?

    O The results are said to be invalid and another type of survey should be administered.

O You should call the parent and teacher and ask questions regarding the Survey. Ask about the child's functioning at home and school.

O Analyze and use other assessment sources used in your evaluation instead of the survey. Although not used in your evaluation, you must make a notation in your report why the survey was not used.

O Interpret both the teacher and parent surveys separately and present the objective results to the special education team.

50. The "stay-put" rule is implemented at what time?

O When "due process" has started.

O When "due process" has completed.

O The "stay put" rule was eliminated with the revised IDEA of 1997.

O When it has been determined that a behavior was a manifestation of a child's disability.

51. At what type of meeting are placement changes made if necessary, eligibility requirements discussed and interventions/modifications are reviewed?

O During the initial staffing meeting with parents and the team.

O During the initial referral meeting

O During the student's annual meeting

O During the assessment and testing phase.

52. When is it considered "best practice" to perform a student evaluation?

O During the student's typical school day.

O When the child is on the playground to see his/her true behavior.

O After you have examined authentic work samples and observations.

O Research has demonstrated that mid-morning is the most effective time.

53. The consumption of large amounts of alcohol during pregnancy can cause?

O Mental Retardation (MR)

O ADHD

O A host of childhood mental illnesses

O Fetal Alcohol Effects (FAE)

54. Autism is considered a?

O Pervasive Developmental Disorder (PDD)

O Obsessive Compulsive disorder (OCD)

O Leading cause of mental retardation

O A genetic disorder that is also linked to heavy drinking during pregnancy.

55. According to Sattler and Kaufman, the most valid and reliable score (s) on mainstream IQ tests such as the WISC is usually the?

O The major cluster or domain score

O The individual subtest scores

O Ipsative score

O The global or full-scale Standard score.

56. According to educational theorists, when fostering intrinsic motivation you should use?

O variable reinforcement

O tangible rewards

O verbal praise

O choice selection

57. Typically, block design subtests on major cognitive assessments mostly evaluate the functioning of the?

O right hemisphere of the brain

O left hemisphere of the brain

O both hemispheres of the brain

O cerebrum

58. If a student's misbehavior increases after the teacher takes away his recess time, this is called?

O Spontaneous negative increase

O   Response cost

O   Negative reinforcement

O   Punishment

59. High school students who have dysgraphia should be given what type of accommodation and/or modification on tests?

O   Extra time

O   Frequent breaks

O   Multiple choice tests

O   A split-half version of the test

60. Which therapeutic method or therapy works best for selective mutism?

O   Reality therapy

O   Cognitive therapy

O   Stimulus fading

O   Flooding

61. A second grade teacher uses the removal of a desirable activity, such as music class, to shape the behavior of his special education students. The teacher does not think other interventions are practical or effective. As the school psychologist, how should you respond?

O   The welfare of the student comes first and the school psychologist has a duty to report the teacher to the principal.

O   It should be explained to the teacher that the method he is using might be working, but will most likely produce short term results if no positive reward is used for compliant behavior.

O   The teacher should be commended for finding something that works. Suggest that feedback should be given to the student when possible.

O   Tell the teacher that he is making the student resentful and that he is fostering external instead of internal behavioral regulation in the student.

62. In regards to the regulation and guidelines for school psychology, a primary difference between the APA and NASP is that?

O   NASP is the only accreditation body for psychologists

O APA does not endorse master or specialist level school psychologists

O There is no difference between APA and NASP guidelines.

O APA only regulates psychiatrists working in schools.

63-65 You completed a comprehensive battery of standardized tests on a student who was referred for special education services. Parents signed permission for your team to complete testing. After the staffing meeting, parents demand that you supply them copies of your protocols.

63. As a licensed school psychologist you should?

O Supply all the necessary copies so you are in compliance with federal law.

O Discreetly state that all necessary information is in the IEP report and review the IEP with the parents.

O You review the protocols with the parents but you do not have to make copies.

O Call the school district's lawyers and have them speak to the parents.

64. Which specific law or case law requires parental "access" to records?

O IDEA

O Kramer v. Kramer

O Brown v. Board of Education

O FERPA

65. If you copy protocols for parents or others, you might be violating what law?

O Federal copyright laws

O FERPA

O Fair Testing and Assessment Act of 1997

O IDEA

66. Executive function primarily impacts?

O Cognitive planning

O Nonverbal learning

    O Spatial reasoning

    O Emotions

67. Which is considered "primary" in crisis intervention?

    O Leadership

    O Community support

    O Measured response

    O Prevention

68. A teacher constantly sends his rowdy students to your office. By mid-year, you are handling several students a week from this one particular teacher. You meet with the teacher in private to discuss the situation. You help him implement a behavioral management plan. Within a few weeks, referrals to you have dropped significantly. What type of consultation model did you use?

    O A direct service model

    O A consultee service model

    O A systems based model

    O The Caplan Model

69. A student is referred to the school psychologist's office because he consistently makes inappropriate comments. What is your first approach to amending this problem?

    O You figure out what is maintaining the behavior and stopping the reinforcement.

    O You set clear expectations for the student and enforce "natural consequences."

    O You perform a quick Functional Behavioral Analysis to determine the antecedent and consequence for the behavior so you can plan an intervention.

    O You tell the teacher to write an office referral for the next incident so there is proper legal documentation.

70. Authentic assessments are different from standardized assessments in which primary way?

O Standardized assessments use statistics to compare a student to a norm group, authentic assessments are more criterion based.

O Authentic assessments are considered informal methods.

O Standardized assessments are more time efficient.

O Authentic assessments are more time efficient.

71. According to many functional behaviorists, what are the primary reasons for most behavior?

O Attention, affiliation and control

O Boredom, opportunity and biological stimulation

O Stimulation, approval and reinforcement

O Praise and approval

72. An upper elementary school student constantly makes poor grades despite his concerted efforts. According to Erik Erikson, if this student does not feel a sense of industry, he will develop problems involving?

O Shame

O Doubt

O Inferiority

O Role confusion

73. A sophomore does not want to break the rules of his school because he does not want to face the disapproval of his strict parents. According to Kohlberg, at which stage of moral development is this student?

O Preconventioal

O Conventional

O Post Conventional

O Assimilation

74. Given a SEM of 6 points, what can be said of a student who receives a Standard Score of 90 on a cognitive assessment?

O The student's range of scores is in the Average to Below Average area.

O The student has an Average score.

O The student has an upper borderline score.

O The student's score is between the 84th and 96th percentile.

75-76 A seventh grade female student has a speech impediment and poor social skills. By the second month of school she is teased by a group of girls to the point the student becomes despondent. Several other students are aware of the teasing, but do not do anything about it. One day, the student writes a detailed note to her teacher that she will kill the teasing students if they do not stop.

75. In previous situation, the school?

O Should immediately counsel all students involved.

O Should mediate the problem with the students involved in the situation.

O Should notify law enforcement immediately.

O Has a duty to warn all parents of the children involved in this situation about the note.

76. In the previous scenario, a school psychologist should?

O Seek to prevent a similar situation by instituting a school wide anti-bullying program

O Use an indirect consultation model to inform the principal about future options.

O Conduct a formal survey to uncover future bullying and harassment problems.

O Perform proactive interventions with targeted classrooms to prevent future acts of bullying.

77. A student is referred to the school psychologist's office for negative self-talk. During your interview, you discover that the student believes she has always had bad luck and bad things just happen to her all the time. This student's belief is a prime example of?

O Negative thinking

O Internal locus of control

O External locus of control

O Low self-concept

78. A caring parent constantly completes the homework for his daughter. Despite suggestions from teachers and school staff, the parent continues to sneak in completed assignments. The parent in this situation is?

    O Instilling in the child learned helplessness

    O Undermining the child's self-concept and self-confidence

    O Breaking the law as outlined in the Tarasoff case.

    O Is modeling negative behavior.

79. A teacher is in the community and sees one of his students at a store. The student has visible marks on his face and arms. The father of this child is known to be verbally aggressive and short tempered. The teacher should?

    O The teacher does not have a duty to notify social services because it is after work hours and not on school grounds.

    O The teacher needs to contact the school social worker immediately.

    O In private, the teacher should ask the student about the marks and then make an informed judgment whether to call social services.

    O As a mandated reporter, the teacher has a duty to notify social services about the marks.

80. A parent comes to you and demands that her son be tested for special education. The student has a history of poor grades and seems to daydream in class. "Best practice" supports what approach?

    O Suggesting interventions before moving ahead with formal testing.

    O Starting the assessment process because parents have legal rights to testing under IDEA law.

    O Tactfully tell the parent to have her son medically evaluated by a pediatrician for attention problems before formal school testing starts.

    O Inform the parent the law gives schools 45 days to complete testing.

81. When should a school psychologist suggest medication for ADHD?

    O After all assessments have been completed.

    O Never

    O Only after securing a release to speak with the student's pediatrician.

    O When the student's behavior impacts other students.

82. A student is asked to dial a phone number while hearing the number for the first time. This is an example of what?

    O Short term memory.

    O Working memory.

    O Information processing

    O Simultaneous processing.

83. A chief characteristic of Autism is?

    O Severe social and communication impairments.

    O Delays in cognitive abilities.

    O Inability to remember spatial and verbal information.

    O Nonverbal learning disability.

84. In regards to suspected child abuse cases, all certified school employees are considered?

    O Not liable if they notify school administration of the suspected abuse.

    O Responsible to report cases of suspected abuse.

    O Government employees are required only to investigate abuse cases.

    O Typically, the school social worker is required to be informed of all child abuse cases.

85. Traumatic brain injury (TBI) in children._____

    O Can cause learning disabilities and attention problems.

    O Is typically not as serious as adult TBI because a child's brain is more malleable than an adult's brain.

    O In most cases will decrease the quality of life of children.

    O Is reflected by significantly higher nonverbal than verbal scores on IQ tests.

86. During a formal assessment, you ask a child to say a word and then manipulate the word's sounds. What are you doing in this task?

    O You are testing for sound discrimination.

    O You are assessing word-sound fluency

O You are evaluating phonemic awareness.

O None of the above answers are valid.

87. A teacher asks for your direct assistance regarding a disruptive student. You agree to observe the child. You discretely sit in the class on three occasions and observe what happens before, during and after the behavior in question. Afterwards, you determine that the student was acting out when the student was near a specific peer. What type of evaluation were you conducting to assist the teacher?

O You were performing a Functional Behavior Assessment

O You were conducting a Formal Evaluation Observation

O You were assessing antecedents and consequences.

O You were evaluating the payoff for the student's behavior.

88. A student has significant difficulty perceiving and reproducing visual symbols accurately. An inability to perceive visual stimuli accurately is typically associated with which part of the brain?

O Visual-spatial cortex

O Parietal lobes

O Frontal lobes

O Occipital lobes

89. Cognitive psychologists hypothesize that the construct of "attention" can be categorized into different types. What are the primary types of attention?

O Selective and fluent

O Focused and fluent

O Selective and sustained

O Sustained and focused

90. When a pre-school child imitates the aggressive behavior of an adult he has just seen in a movie, what is this called?

O Modeling

O Latent aggression

O   Observational learning

O   Behavioral dysregulation

91.   Who is the theorist largely responsible for studying aggression in children and conducting experiments using a "Bo-Bo" doll?

O   B.F. Skinner

O   Albert Switzer

O   Albert Bandura

O   Carl Jung

92.   A colleague asks you to review a journal article that describes several studies and experiments. You are specifically asked to discern the strongest correlation coefficient from the following. Which one depicts the strongest correlation?

O   .97

O   -.98

O   .100

O   -.250

93-95. In an experiment, you want to examine the effect background music has on learning. You form two groups. One group studies with soft background music, while the other group studies in a quiet area.

93.   The group exposed to background music is called?

O   The experimental group

O   The independent group

O   The control group

O   The dependent variable

94.   The group not exposed to background music is called?

O   The experimental group

O   The independent group

O   The control group

O   The dependent variable

95. In the experiment, "music" is considered what?

    O Experimental variable

    O Manipulation variable

    O Independent variable

    O Dependent variable

96. When you assess a student for special services, "best practice" suggests that you?

    O Use at least two valid standardized measures before identifying a disorder or disability.

    O Secure a second opinion from another school psychologists before formally identifying a disorder.

    O Use both valid formal and informal assessments to base your decisions.

    O Do not use informal assessments.

97. Aphasia is normally associated with what type of problem?

    O A speech/language disturbance

    O A visual-motor disturbance

    O An inability to read

    O A difficulty with math or quantitative problem solving

98. A student employs a problem solving strategy that reduces the number of options or alternative she must consider. This student is utilizing what type of problem solving technique?

    O Deduction

    O Successive processing

    O Logical reasoning

    O A heuristic

99. A teacher asks you to assist him with a student who has reading difficulties. You suggest that the student think out loud and predict outcomes of selected paragraphs. Most likely, these suggestions are to improve the student's?

○ Reading fluency

○ Decoding skills

○ Comprehension skills

○ Encoding skills

100. During a structured interview, you notice that the interviewee is well groomed and has a quick, but polite sense of humor. Care must be taken that your assessment results are not tainted by what psychological phenomenon?

○ Halo effect

○ Observer bias distortion

○ Perceptual-bias effect

○ Skalski effect

101. You work as a school psychologist for a rural school district. Budget problems and personnel shortages are persistent in your district. The principal of your school informs you not to make recommendations for parents to seek community counseling services for their children. Additionally, the principal informs you that you must only conduct group counseling sessions to improve your time effectiveness. Based on ethics and best practices, how do you respond?

○ Given the practical concerns of the situation, you should comply with the principal's directives.

○ You explain your ethical obligations to the principal, but still comply with the directives.

○ You notify the principal that you cannot completely comply with the directives because some situations demand certain actions.

○ You consult with the district's attorney and bring the matter before the school board.

102. Curriculum based measurement (CBM) enables a teacher to?

○ Continuously monitor progress and adjust goals as necessary.

○ Compare a student's performance to his/her norm group to determine what is typical.

O Provide evidence of progress in a given curriculum.

O Determine if a curriculum is reliable and valid.

103. When meeting with a child for the first time in a counseling meeting, a school psychologist should first secure?

O Consent from the principal or school administration.

O Informed consent from parents.

O Consent from the administration and parents.

O If licensed by a state government to work in public schools, no consent is necessary, but is considered appropriate.

104. A school district is mandated to formally assess children of all ages with suspected disabilities. According to educational law, this previous statement is known as?

O No reject

O Child find

O Inclusion

O Exclusion

105. Which standardized cognitive assessment is largely based on the Luria Model and the PASS (Planning, Attention, Simultaneous and Successive) theory?

O The Differential Ability Scales (DAS)

O The WISC-IV

O Stanford-Binet-IV

O The Cognitive Assessment System (CAS)

106. A counseling approach that embraces the idea that behavior is guided by one's self-image, subjective perceptions and the need for growth toward personal goals is called?

O Psychodynamic Counseling

O Behaviorism

O Humanistic Counseling

O Cognitive-Behavioral Counseling

107. The Catell-Horn theory of intelligence forms the basis for many current cognitive tests. According to this theory, intelligence can be divided into which two primary domains?

　O　Verbal-Performance

　O　Neurological-Cognitive

　O　Cognitive-Behavioral

　O　Fluid-Crystallized

108. NASP generally recommends how many school psychologists per student population?

　O　1 per 1000 students

　O　2 per 1000 students

　O　1 per school

　O　1 per 2000 students

109-111. An upper elementary school student is referred to the special team for unusual social and egocentric behavior. As a school psychologist, you first conduct an observation of the student and interview the teacher. Your inquiry reveals that the young boy has an uncanny ability to remember detailed facts about WWII military planes. You also find the child has motor clumsiness, abnormalities in inflection when he speaks and difficulty in social situations. However, you note that he has a few friends and engages in group activities without external assistance.

109. Based on the presenting symptoms, you decide to formally test the student for which disability?

　O　Autism

　O　Nonverbal Learning Disorder (NVLD)

　O　Social Processing Disorder (SPD)

　O　Asperger's Syndrome

110. Parents have given you signed permission to help the student in the previous scenario. You decide that social skills training is the best initial approach. Which of the following best reflects social skills training?

　O　Self-awareness, positive reinforcement and social praise

　O　Direct instruction, modeling and coaching

O Metacognitive training, operant techniques and active listening

O Perspective taking, response cost and social praise

111. Your team feels that the student in the previous example needs special education services. In making the decision to offer the student special services, your team must demonstrate what critical finding?

O The child has a diagnosable disability as outlined in the DSM-IV-R

O Your testing results must show a significant and verifiable processing deficit.

O The child's behavior has a significant impact on his social development and classroom performance.

O Standardized testing must document that the student has a score that is at least two Standard Deviations below the Mean.

112. When conducting a Functional Behavioral Analysis, which primary characteristic(s) of the behavior is important to document and analyze?

O The frequency, intensity and duration of the target behavior.

O How many times the behavior presents itself when the antecedent is known.

O What reinforces the behavior.

O What triggers the behavior.

113. According to J. Sattler, approximately what percentage of the student population has some form of learning disability?

O 3–5%

O 5–8%

O 10–15%

O 15–20%

114. On common cognitive assessments such as the WISC-IV, what is the generally accepted Standard IQ score for "gifted" students?

O A Standard Score above 115

O A Standard Score above 120

O A Standard Score above 130

O A Standard Score above 140

115. A student who has a severe vision impairment is granted a school waiver that excuses her from taking the state's annual assessment test. The parents of this student demand that the school accommodate her so that she can take the test. According to the law, what is the school's responsibility?

O The school must fulfill the needs of the student so she can complete the standardized state test.

O The school is under no legal obligation, but ethically should make the appropriate accommodations.

O The school should keep to its original plan and fully excuse the child from the test.

O The school's decision to spend resources to accommodate the student depends on whether the student has a 504 or IEP.

116. Considering the following statements regarding school violence, which statement is <u>not</u> true?

O There is a general profile of a "school shooter" that all school psychologist should know.

O Most perpetrators of school violence have been bullied in the past.

O Incidents of targeted school violence at school are rarely impulsive.

O Most attackers engaged in behaviors that indicated concerns by others.

117. The most effective intervention(s) for children with learning disabilities are?

O Cognitive and behavioral

O Multifaceted/Multimodal

O Linguistic

O neuropsychological

118. The term "running record" is usually associated with this type of observational recording?

O Interval recording

O Narrative recording

O Event recording

O Ratings recording

119. What is NASP's position regarding home-schooling?

O NASP does not endorse the concept of home-schooling due to the lack of quality assurance and professional instruction provided to children.

O NASP believes in collaboration between parents of home schooled children and the public schools.

O Home schooled children are most at risk for social developmental delays.

O Psycho-educational assessments are usually not provided to children who are not enrolled and attending public schools.

120. The ability to analyze and synthesize several pieces of information is related to which type of cognitive processing?

O Sequential

O Spatial

O Metacognitive

O Simultaneous

Appendix

Models of Basic Information Processing (Cognitive Psychology)

I. Basic model

Information (Input)----------Central Processing----------Expressive (Output)

II. Complex Model

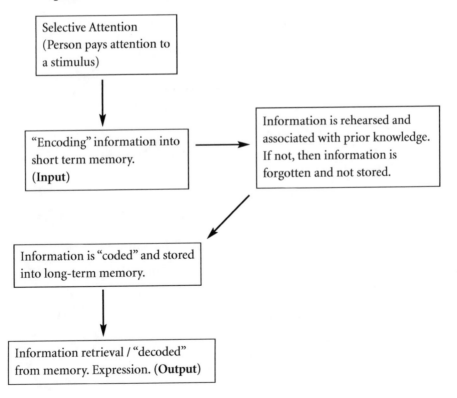

Selective Attention
(Person pays attention to
a stimulus)

"Encoding" information into
short term memory.
(Input)

Information is rehearsed and
associated with prior knowledge.
If not, then information is
forgotten and not stored.

Information is "coded" and stored
into long-term memory.

Information retrieval / "decoded"
from memory. Expression. (Output)

Note—The average person can hold approximately 7–8 bits of information in short-term memory (what is sometimes called *transient memory*). Short-term memory should not be confused with working memory. In working memory, one must perform an activity while holding ideas, thoughts and information *online*.

> A breakdown or problem can occur on any level of the information-processing model. For example, people may have difficulty learning because they are not properly "encoding" the information. On the other hand, people may have properly encoded the information and understand concepts, but cannot retrieve (decode) the details of the data.

Basic Neuropsychological/Neuroanatomical Concepts

Lobes of the Cerebral Cortex (Neo Cortex).

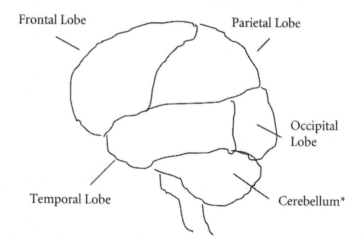

I. The Cerebral Cortex is the higher order "thinking" brain.

Frontal lobe—Manager of the brain. Associated with "executive functioning." Controls goal-directed behavior and cognitive planning.

Temporal lobe—Language Center. Processes auditory information. Wernicke's area is in this section of the brain

Occipital lobe—Processes visual information

Parietal lobe—Somatosensory area. Processes bodily sensation and motor functions. Also integrates some information.

*Cerebellum—This area of the brain is not considered part of the Cerebral Cortex, but rather part of the Hindbrain. The Cerebellum controls muscle tone, balance and skilled movement.

II. The deeper structures of the brain contain the *Limbic System* which is implicated in emotions, motivation and emotional disorders.

Important parts of the Limbic System (Emotional Brain)

Hippocampus—Implicated in forming strong emotional memories and learning.

Amygdala—Emotional center. Regulates emotional valence. Approach/avoidance.

Hypothalamus—Largely influences sex, primary emotions, sleep, and hunger. Associated with homeostasis. Brain's thermostat.

Thalamus—Sensory "relay" station. Most sensory information such as visual and auditory information is initially evaluated through this area.

Additional Notes

Neurochemicals (brain chemicals)

> **Dopamine**—is involved in producing positive moods and feelings. Associated with reward seeking and novelty seeking. Implicated in Parkinson's disease and ADHD.

> **Endorphin**—A natural opiate similar to morphine. Released to moderate pain.

> **Serotonin**—Helps regulate relaxation, sleep and mood. Implicated in clinical depression.

Damage to Broca's or Wernicke's area can cause speech and language difficulties known as *aphasias.*

Broca's area is located within the frontal lobe. Wernicke's is located in the temporal lobe. Both are associated with dyslexia and other learning disabilities.

The Reticular Activating System (RAS)—is located in the primitive hindbrain and is responsible for cortical tone and arousal. The RAS keeps the brain active and alert.

The Corpus Callosum is a brain structure that connects both right and left cortical hemispheres so information can be exchanged and integrated. The Corpus Callosum is a communication line between the two halves of the brain.

The right hemisphere of the brain is typically associated with nonverbal and novel information processing. Visual-spatial data, facial recognition and patterns are processed in this area. Performance-based tasks on cognitive assessments sometimes tap this area.

The left hemisphere is associated with processing information that is familiar. Speech, language, writing and calculations are processed in this part.

It is important to keep in mind that right-left hemisphere specialization is an *over-simplification of brain functioning.* New research in this area is quickly dispelling long held beliefs.

There are several different types of memory (visual, auditory, procedural, etc.). Memory is not located in one particular area of the brain, but diffused throughout. However, there are important brain structures such as the hippocampus that are important to the creation of certain types of memories.

Working memory is a key type of memory necessary for learning and performing tasks. It is also implicated in some behavioral disorders.

Digit span type of tests usually tap simple auditory memory and attention. Digits forward taps simple short-term memory, while digits backwards taps working memory to a degree.

Quick Reference of Major Psychological Theories

Psychodynamic—Behavior is strongly influenced by forces within one's personality which are usually unconscious. People are controlled by impulses, desires and conflicts that need to be resolved. Early experiences (0–5 years) are vital to development. Freudian "stage" theory that examines the "id, ego and superego."

Humanistic—Behavior is influenced by one's self-concept and subjective perceptions. There is a "need" for personal growth. See Maslow's hierarchy of needs and Carl Rogers' work on human connections.

Behavioristic—Behavior is shaped by consequences and the environment. This is a mechanistic view of behavior and learning. People learn by associating events to outcomes. Strong emphasis on scientific data collection of observable behavior. Basis for FBA. Associated with BF Skinner and Pavlov.

Cognitive—Concerned with a person's perception and thinking about events and people. Behavior is shaped by how one processes information and the values/beliefs stemming from one's thinking. People can learn by <u>observing</u> others. Consequences do not necessarily have to happen to the person for learning to take place as seen in the Behavioristic theory. Associated with schema or cognitive maps (See Albert Bandura's work).

Neuro/Biopsychological—Behavior is heavily influenced by physiological, chemical and biological processes. Biochemistry and neurochemicals are prominent features of this theory. Behavior can sometimes by reduced down to the cellular or neuronal level (reductionistic theory). See works by Dan Goleman (*Emotional Intelligence*) and J. LeDoux.

Other important theories—

Theory of the Mind—An understanding that other people have different thoughts, perspectives and feelings. This theory is sometimes associated with Autism.

Social Comparison Theory—People use their peer group to evaluate their own opinions, feelings, actions and abilities.

Attribution Theory—People interpret and attribute their emotions to events, which in turns shapes their behavior and thinking. Attribution is largely based on cognitive theory.

The Normal Distribution of Human Traits/Bell Curve

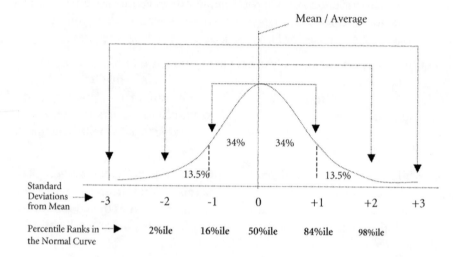

Note: > Approximately 68% of all people fall within 1 Standard Deviation from the mean (34% + 34% = 68)

> Percentiles (listed on the bottom) are not percentages and are not equal interval measurements like Standard Scores.

Helpful Resources

The following list of resources is obviously not exhaustive. However, even a modest internet search will quickly return an avalanche of websites. Due to the overwhelming amount of sources, both relevant and irrelevant, I purposely limited the amount of additional information. Below are some of the most helpful resources.

➢ *Best Practices in School Psychology IV* (or most recent edition). National Association of School Psychologists. (Read Abstracts mostly, but read chapters that cover information in your areas of weakness.)

➢ www.nasponline.org This is NASP's website. Read position papers and other relevant information.

➢ www.apa.org./about/division/div16html This is the American Pyschological Association (APA) division of school psychology (Division 16).

➤ www.schoolpsychologist.net This is one of the best websites devoted to most topics related to school psychology. Additionally, this website has an impressive list of links and other resources.

➤ Jerome Sattler; (2002). *Assessment of Children Behavioral and Clinical Applications-Fourth Edition.* San Diego: Jerome Sattler Publisher.

➤ Jerome Sattler, (2002). *Cognitive Assessment of Children-Fourth Edition.* San Diego: Jerome Sattler Publisher.

➤ Randy Kamphaaus, (2001). *Clinical Assessment of Children and Adolescent Intelligence-Second Edition.* Needham Heights, MA:Allyn and Bacon.

➤ Prout, T., & Brown, T. (1999). *Counseling and Psychotherapy with Children and Adolescents. Theory and Practice for School and Clincial Setting-Third Edition.* NY: John Wiley & Sons.

Answers to Practice Test

Answer Key: On the practice test, the first answer choice for each question corresponds to "A", the second choice to "B", the third choice to "C" and the fourth answer choice to "D".

1. D
2. A
3. B
4. A
5. B
6. D
7. C
8. B
9. B
10. B
11. A
12. C
13. D
14. A
15. D
16. A
17. C
18. A
19. B
20. A
21. D
22. D
23. A
24. A
25. A

26. B
27. A
28. C
29. D
30. C
31. B
32. A
33. A
34. C
35. A
36. B
37. B
38. A
39. C
40. B
41. B
42. C
43. C
44. A
45. C
46. B
47. B
48. A
49. B
50. A
51. C
52. A
53. D
54. A
55. D
56. D
57. A
58. C
59. C
60. C
61. B
62. B
63. C
64. D
65. A

66. A
67. D
68. B
69. C
70. A
71. A
72. C
73. B
74. A
75. D
76. A
77. C
78. B
79. D
80. A
81. B
82. B
83. A
84. B
85. A
86. C
87. A
88. D
89. C
90. A
91. C
92. B
93. A
94. C
95. C
96. C
97. A
98. D
99. C
100. A
101. C
102. A
103. B
104. B
105. D

106. C
107. D
108. A
109. D
110. B
111. C
112. A
113. C
114. C
115. A
116. A
117. B
118. B
119. B
120. D

About the Author

Peter Thompson was born in a small town called Lafayette, Louisiana. After majoring in behavioral studies and graduating from the University of Louisiana, Peter moved to Los Angeles where he worked in a residential treatment facility for dual diagnosed adults. Over the intervening years, the author accumulated valuable experience as a public school math teacher, service provider for severely handicapped adults and a writer of various newspaper articles.

Peter then moved to Austin to study at the University of Texas. After completing his master's degree in psychology and service in the Army Reserves, he moved to Denver with his wife. While working in multiple schools, the author earned his specialist degree and licensure in school psychology. Peter is currently employed as a licensed school psychologist for Douglas County Schools in Colorado.

0-595-33527-6

Made in the USA